Voice of Hope

by
Chris Fife

© 9/4/2017

Table of Contents

Introduction

We now live in very trying times. There are wars and conflicts all around the world. The economic balance of the world is just holding on a thread. There are real threats such as global climate change, nuclear war, starvation, disease, and economic collapse.

Most of the governments of the world contain corruption and criminal intent. The extent of our life expectancy has reached its limit and is starting to decline. No one can really predict what will happen tomorrow, next year, or in thirty years. The only consensus among experts is that terrible things will happen.

Now that I got some of the gloom and doom out of the way. The intent of this book is not to talk about the apocalypse or to foretell the end of the world. I am neither a prophet or a scientist. There have been several books written on these things. My intent is to bring hope and brightness into our lives of a future we are not scared for our grandchildren to live in.

This book will talk of the bad things in the world today, but it will also talk of the good and the possible future we can make if we work together in making it happen. I am just a simple average person, a writer, a teacher, a father, a husband, a mormon, and a citizen of the world. I write this book to wake up the politicians, the government officials, the teachers, the heads of state, those in authority to do something to start making change happen.

Chapter One: Government

People around the world are upset with the corruption they see in governments. They find men and women who are incompetent leading their countries. There is much debate over which form of government is the better than the other.

In the past governments consisted of kings and queens that had absolute rule over the people. These kings and queens would have followers who they trusted and gave favor to in the form of land and wealth. In return the nobles would provide protection. The rest of the people were expected to work and give a portion of what they had to the king. The king in turn would make sure his people were protected. This system of government became known as autocracy where one person rules the land.

The people of the world relied on their king and hoped they had a good king who would treat them well. If they had a wicked or harsh king they would be miserable. They may even have an insane king who was unpredictable in his behavior. Civil rights were non-existent, unless the king felt like granting them to his citizens.

Then came the Greeks who thought of a new type of government where the people had a say in what happened. This form of government known as democracy allowed people to have power in the government. This works great for a small town, but is difficult for a large city or country unless the people elect representatives to give them a voice in the government. The voting of representatives in a government is a republic which most of the countries are today.

After the Greeks came the Romans who followed the example of the Greeks with a Senate and the involvement of the Roman citizens in the government. Rome had a series of emperors who seized the power over the senate and made it an autocracy and then the government collapsed. This collapse resulted the government being replaced with the kings and queens of the middle ages. It wasn't until England started to give power to the nobles instead of the king that parliament was established and later the United States of America with its constitution gave power back to the people.

Since the United States Constitution many countries have followed its model in the form of a democratic government. The problem is not in the form of government itself, but in how it is implemented. I will attempt to explain some of the main points of the problem in politics in the United States.

Problems

The first problem with politics in the United States is the separation of classes and the inequality of elections. In order to be elected to a public office in the United States you have to first be wealthy and second be popular among the right people, the elite people. This means you need to become best of friends to the democrats or the republicans. In order to be elected you need to have the backing of a major party and the money to campaign. The major problem with this is that there are a lot of favors going on within the parties to wealthy individuals and organizations in order to be elected.

There has been talk about campaign reform and the money involved. You may have heard about special interest groups and the corruption that is involved with a group supporting a candidate and then getting a favor from the candidate after being elected. It is hard to really say the people being elected to represent the people actually represents the people. They represent their party, the lobbyists who supported them, and the wealthy minority of the nation.

The candidates will discuss major issues in debates against their opponents and talk about how they will fix the nation's problems, but are they really going to represent the people and do what is the greater good for the country? Public office is the essence of serving the people. Are these candidates really going to serve the people, or only those who got them elected? The president by the very oath he or she takes defends the constitution which is the supreme law of the land to protect the rights all of the people the president serves.

It is difficult at best to choose public servants who are not bias towards a cause or a group given the current status of elections. This is not just an American problem. It is worldwide. Just about every country that has a democratic election process has political parties and groups that support a candidate to be elected. These groups gain control of the power of the country.

The United States which started out as a democracy is now an oligarchy where one group has the power in the country. This group which is either democrat or republican attempts to push their agenda on the country. It could be the democrats pushing abortion or same sex marriage. It could be the republicans allowing for deregulation of gun laws and stricter immigration enforcement. There is some checks and balances with both parties being in the government, but there are many Americans who do not feel they believe in either parties platform.

George Washington gave a warning voice to what is happening in America and the world today. "The alternate domination of one faction over another, sharpened by the spirit of revenge, natural to party dissension, which in different ages and countries has perpetrated the most horrid enormities, is itself a frightful despotism. But this leads at length to a more formal and permanent despotism. The disorders and miseries, which result, gradually incline the minds of men to seek security and repose in the absolute power of an individual; and sooner or later the chief of some prevailing faction, more able or more fortunate than his competitors, turns this disposition to the purposes of his own elevation, on the ruins of Public Liberty."

The very thing the United States stands for and was founded on has been trampled on by political parties and special interest groups. The corruption that exists the world wide comes from groups that are attempting to push their interests over the interests of the common good of a people, a nation, and the world we live in.

George Washington further warned about parties. As you read this think about what is happening today and how this very statement rings true.

"The common and continual mischief's [sic] of the spirit of party are sufficient to make it the interest and the duty of a wise people to discourage and restrain it. It serves always to distract the public councils and enfeeble the public administration. It agitates the community with ill founded jealousies and false alarms, kindles the animosity of one part against another, foments occasionally riot and insurrection. It opens the door to foreign influence and corruption, which find a facilitated access to the government itself through the channels of party passion."

Political parties in the United States and around the world are ripping apart the very thing freedom was founded upon. The democrats and republicans in America are divided over the issues and fight to gain control of the government. Each party has its own agenda and its own set of values which often clash with that of the other party. I am not sure either party has the best interest of the people of the United States. Even the major issues they fight over are blurred and little if anything is accomplished.

Americans have become frustrated with the current politics of Washington. There seems to be only two choices to represent the country and these choices are not desirable nor do they represent the best of America. Should Americans blindly follow candidates and a party they currently belong to? There is nothing in the constitution that says the people need to be republican or democrat. It does not say a person running for office needs to belong to a particular party.

Our government was founded upon the principles that the people should have a say in the government and the government should protect the rights of the people. It seems like neither of these are currently being honored by the government, because of the political parties we have. Should we have more political parties? Should we replace those we have with something better?

George Washington warned that parties just cause trouble. Political parties should not have as much power as they do. Even if the two current parties divided the power in Washington and in each state it still would cause a lot of problems. There needs to be more of a neutral position on political control. We should not do away with political parties they give us a healthy debate over issues and allow the country to examine issues with different perspectives. The problem is how much control and blind follow we have in following a party and the candidates it chooses. There needs to be a better alternative to what we now have. There needs to be measures taken to limit the power of the parties.

Solutions

There are many solutions that can work. The trick is to get people to take action and do them. We need to break tradition and come up with a better way of doing things. The first would be the election process. Instead of wealthy people raising millions of dollars and advertising their candidacy there needs to be an independent election committee giving every candidate an equal chance at winning the race. Just think if we took all of the money in elections and added it to helping fund research, putting it into education, or helping the poor in America. It sickens me when there is hundreds of millions of dollars spent on campaigns each year to elect someone who is most likely not the best candidate.

Candidates regardless of political party should have equal media attention, equal coverage, and be able to debate with each other. There needs to be a selection process for candidates so that we do not have hundreds of people throwing their hat into the ring. The selection process should involve a series of tests, background checks, and qualifications in order to be able to be the best we have to offer to represent us.

The American people need to be well informed about each candidate with community meetings, informational mailings, and websites independent of the candidates giving people a non-bias look at who to vote for. We need to break tradition and elect people who are not supported by the democrats or the republicans.

The candidates once elected need to drop their allegiance to either party and focus on representing the people. The common good should be the top priority. Politicians need to be courageous enough to stand up and be counted for doing the right thing. Too many politicians are spending their energy trying to satisfy the demands of special interest groups.

They need to be held accountable for their behavior as a politician and in their private lives. Just like all of the rest of us who are evaluated by our employers for job performance, politicians need to be elevated by the voters at least once a year. It can send a clear message to elected officials the direction they need to take and make them accountable for their actions.

Elected officials should not be given a salary for their work as public servants. An elected position in the very spirit of its office should be one of service to the people and not a paid position where they can sit by and do very little and get paid for it. If elected offices did not get paid and thought more of their office as a community service position they might treat the office with more respect and do things that are more in the spirit of the office. It would also send a clear message to the world that our leaders are serving the people.

All elected officials need to be people of good moral character with the highest of standards. They are models for the rest of the people in the country. Children should be able to look up to them and see them as people they can be more like. People in the country think more about leaders like Abraham Lincoln, and Theodore Roosevelt. Men with very high ideals and moral fiber. We need more leaders like them to continue to lead the nation into the future. The standards for public office need to be set high and those elected held to those standards. If this does not occur the very fabric of society will collapse and corruption will enter into every level of government.

Call to Action

We as a people need to demand change and not just sit idly by and allow our nations government to melt into oblivion. It needs to start on a local level with people who are the best candidates encouraged to run for office and being elected no matter if the candidate is a republican, democrat, or an independent. Campaign reform needs to take place starting in states where independent committees run the election and the candidates are given equal opportunity to run for office.

Chapter Two: A House Divided

Abraham Lincoln in a speech he gave in Illinois in 1858 when he was running for US Senate spoke of the issue of Slavery. It is now known as the House Divided speech. Lincoln lost the race to Steven A. Douglas and at the time many people believed Lincoln's speech was too controversial. America at the time was divided between free states and slave states and there was an atmosphere of compromise to satisfy the issue of slavery.

Lincoln in his wisdom quoted the Bible Mark 3:25. There are several other passages in the Bible that say the same thing. Lincoln continued in his speech saying, "The country cannot be half slave and half free." The same message applies today.

The universal truth is that you cannot be divided between two masters. You cannot serve two masters. You will end up serving one and hating the other. This is also from the scriptures. (Luke 16:13) We live in a time when there are so many things that divide the country.

Marijuana Legalization

One of the major issues facing the country that is dividing it is marijuana legalization. Just like when the country was divided over slavery. There are those states where marijuana is legal and those where it is not. There are people who are for it and those against. It has become a battleground and will increase as more people take a stand. This can be a dangerous area where the country is divided as people who are almost religiously worshiping marijuana are pushing its recreational use and those opposed to it are fighting it like as the new plague.

There really is not enough research done to have a clear picture as to the effects of marijuana use and if it could be considered a viable medical drug. It is a dangerous slippery slope of introducing something to the general public without the research to back it. If there was any other drug made it would go through years of research and clinical trials before being placed on the market, and would never be considered for recreational use.

There is a lot of arguments on both sides of the issue both with their merits. But the bottom line would be how it divides the country. Some could argue that marijuana and drugs is the new slavery. How many people could honestly say that they can avoid using a drug they have been taking for years without going through rehab. They are a slave to its addictive properties. The division of the drug issue could be something that may end in another civil war. If marijuana is made legal in the United States what would be next; cocaine, heroine, or meth. What will be the affects of nationwide use of marijuana? What would happen to the rising generation of children exposed to this?

We only have to look to Colorado or some of the other states who have made marijuana legal. More children are using it and some have had to be hospitalized because of it. There is no benefits from the legalization except for the money it generates because of the addictive qualities. Just like how the tobacco companies and food industry makes money from caffeine and nicotine products.

We might want to ask the question; why are we making it legal to use? Is it for profit? At what cost to society will it bring? Just look at how much money is spent on the trouble alcohol has caused and the untold deaths tobacco has caused. Now we have another substance we have to deal with.

Same Sex Marriage

Before the Supreme Court ruled in favor of same sex marriage the states were divided on the issue. Many people are still divided on the issue. There is still a lot of bigotry and prejudice against same gender attraction. This is only a fraction of the issue. There is no doubt that as a people we should not deny rights to people based on their sexual orientation. However, when it comes to marriage there is a larger argument that involves fundamental religious and cultural beliefs.

Just because a law is put into place it does not mean everyone agrees with the law or that the law is just. Which places a lot of people in an uncomfortable position when it comes to same sex marriage. There becomes a conflict between the first amendment right to practice religion and the Supreme Courts decision to allow same sex marriage.

Those who argue for same sex marriage are fighting for the rights of gay people to express their love to one another through marriage. They feel like they should be able to marry each other regardless of their sexual orientation. Many people agree there should not be any prejudice when it comes to their rights.

Those who argue against same sex marriage believe marriage should be only between a man and a woman. This argument has a religious basis as well as a traditional basis where the family unit comes. A marriage involving a man and woman can produce children and be raised in a traditional family. This cannot take place in a same sex marriage unless the couple adopts children or in the case of a lesbian couple one or both partners becomes pregnant artificially.

Marriage in general is being attacked. More people are not getting married or having temporary marriages that end in divorce. This is changing the course of relationships and how children are raised. Many children end up being raised by single parents who have multiple relationships. Children end up in an unstable environment changing from one moment to the next without the proper education that is essential in the home to be successful.

Health Care

Americans pay more for health care than most of the nations on Earth. According to a 2017 NUMBEO health care index the United States ranks 27 in the world. The country is divided over the idea of how health care should be run. The costs are continually going up and the quality is not getting any better.

Sure there are continual advancements in medical technology and medicines, but many health care professionals are overworked. Patients are often treated like numbers instead of people. Gone are the days when doctors make house calls and they have a more personalized relationship with the family. The healing process required more of a personalized touch than just issuing medicine to people and forgetting about them.

The main issues involving health care are costs, quality, and accessibility. Many Americans do not want national health care. The fact of the matter is that we do have national health care, but the way we go about doing it is insanely costly.

We get a lot of money taken out of our checks that goes toward medicare and for health insurance. This amount can be well into the hundreds of dollars for a family. On top of this amount we have to pay for deductibles and copays. So an average family could end up paying thousands of dollars in medical expenses a year and have relatively few visits to the hospital. Even after you pay a lot of money to be covered by insurance, it is possible that you could end up owing ten thousand dollars or more because of deductibles you have to pay first, or medical expenses your insurance will not cover.

People in the government have thought they new the answer and have tried to fix this problem. The affordable health care act under president Obama did anything, but make health care affordable. It required everyone to have health insurance, despite not being able to afford it and forced employers to give health insurance to their employees. In some aspects it raised the costs of health care.

The quality of health care is not getting better. Many health care professionals are overworked, because there are not enough of them to cover the amount of people who need medical attention. Many of the practices or procedures are not covered by insurance so doctors cannot practice wholistic medicine. Insurance may not cover things like acupuncture or herbal medicines. Insurance companies also do not cover preventative practices such as eating healthy or exercise. Many do penalize poor practices such as smoking and excessive drinking, but a lot of people can lie about these things on forms.

Accessibility to health care is marginal when it comes to availability to medical services. In most areas people are minutes from a medical facility and they are able to access emergency services by calling 911. But there are still rural areas that are hours away from adequate medical service including 911. There are also areas where the only 24 hours service is the emergency room which is further away. Medical services tend to be lacking in many of the poor neighborhoods with waiting rooms packed with people waiting to be treated.

Social Economic Status

The greatest divide in the United States is social economic status. There is a huge divide between those in poverty and the wealthy of the nation. This divide is often shaped by the communities and neighborhoods of cities and states. A person living in the poor neighborhoods of places like Detroit or Chicago have fewer opportunities than those living in wealthy neighborhoods in upper state New York and the New England states.

This divide includes education, health care, career opportunities, and living conditions. People living in poverty get less of an education, are more likely to be unhealthy, and are more likely to live in an atmosphere of abuse, violence, and criminal behavior. Those who live in wealth have access to better education, health care, and safer neighborhoods. Many people follow a cycle where they remain poor because of the lack of opportunities. While wealthy people tend to remain in a state of wealth.

People who are out of work and unhappy with their social economic status will take it out on those closest to them. This is generally family, friends, and their neighborhood in the form of riots. This violence can spill over into nearby neighborhoods and grow in intensity.

Race

America is still a country divided by race. Racism is still roaming the country with so called, "Hate groups". They continue to organized groups of people who spread racist propaganda on the internet, newspapers, and in meetings. These racist groups have caused a lot of violence in the past and will continue to create problems in the future. Fortunately Americans have law on their side and can settle many injustices through the courts.

However, when there tends to be a great deal of people belonging to a certain group in an area. Those whose are suppose to uphold the law, may be the ones breaking it. This has happened a lot in certain areas of the south. Today this is happening throughout the country in pockets where hate groups are established.

Anti-Federalist

There is a growing number of people who are dissatisfied with how the federal government handles things. People are upset how the government will take land from a state and make it a national monument. Some are upset about how the government runs the land which they believe is part of their family land. Many people throughout the United States simply wants the federal government to stay out of things states are doing.

If we take a look at many of the areas that divide the nation it is the federal governments involvement or lack thereof that creates more of a divide. Marijuana is an illegal drug according to the federal government, yet several states have made it legal. You can buy it in Colorado and get arrested for possession in Kansas. Federal agents can go into many of these states where marijuana is legal and arrest people, because they are breaking federal law. The federal government in part is ignoring the marijuana issue.

In the case of same sex marriage many states outlawed it and even changed their constitutions to define marriage. It was the Supreme Court that changed this so marriages are legal in all states. This means that the federal government overturned many laws in several states.

The federal government has tackled health care, poverty, and race issues with very little success. The federal government has the power to do a lot of good in the United States, but it also has the power to cause a lot of trouble and could shatter the fragile balance we have in preventing a major division that would result in another civil war. The possibility of another civil war is very slime. But there could be major unrest and even a point where martial law could be declared. There is not enough opposition to create a major group in opposition to federal authority.

The question is about how unified is the United States? Is there enough opposition and division in a state like Texas to bring about separation and the creation of a new nation? Will local law enforcement and the national guard be able to handle wide scale rioting and violence?

It is scary seeing what is happening around the world in places like Syria and Venezuela. No one would want the country to get to this point. What if the police were overwhelmed? Would the country turn to chaos and anarchy in the streets with neighbor fighting neighbor? In New Orleans after hurricane Katrina there was widespread looting and violence. There have been several places throughout the

United States where people go to the streets in riots causing millions of dollars in damage, injuring, and killing other people. Organized gangs have made neighborhoods their territory where they sell drugs and create an atmosphere of terror through the violence they promote.

Americans should not be worried so much about terrorist attacks or foreign invasion. The greatest threat is within our own boarders. It is scary to think of all of the guns private citizens own. There are enough weapons in our neighborhoods to create civil unrest that would rival that of Syria. The number of weapons private citizens own can fall into the hands of gangs, hate groups, and people who will take law into their own hands when the police are not their to protect them.

There is plenty of things to be concerned about in the United States to make people stand up and take notice. Yet it is often what is happening in other places around the world that is in the news. Each president focuses on terrorists and the threat other countries may pose to the United States. This tends to be a little misdirected since more people die from domestic violence and gang violence than all of the people who died from terrorist attacks or the resent wars we have fought.

According to a CNN article they found that from 2001-2014 there were 3,415 death caused by terrorism including from 9/11. In that same period of time there were 440,095 deaths that were caused by firearms in the United States. President Obama was one of the only presidents to make an issue of how violent our country really is. The deaths included accidents and suicide. America is divided over the concept of gun control and the 2nd amendment. The debate over this alone creates a very divided nation.

Americans are divided over several issues not just the ones mentioned. People are divided over abortion, sports, political ideas, and many other cultural traditions. One thing that does make America great is the freedom to be different and to disagree with other people about what they believe in. It is healthy to have some opposition and to challenge the positions people take. What is not okay, is the violence associated with the division, and the lack of tolerance and bigotry that comes with it.

Call to Action

We have an opportunity to come closer together and be in harmony like no other period in history. The time for ignorance is past. People should recognize the gift of free agency and choice everyone has and be more tolerant of other people's beliefs and lifestyles. It is important that we do not force our beliefs and lifestyle on others and not allow the government to force people to do things they do not want to do.

Marijuana needs to be deglamorized and placed in its corrected place. If it does have some medical application treat it as medicine and not something to have a good time with. We already have enough troubles with alcohol, tobacco, and caffeine. We do not need another pleasure seeking drug that will create societal problems. If it does achieve the status of being legal it needs to be contained to small areas, with strict regulation, and extremely high taxes.

Same sex marriage needs to have a different designation. It is difficult for many to be able to define it as a traditional marriage which results in children and a traditional family. Same sex marriage could open up a wave of non-traditional pleas for marriage such as marriage to pets, objects, family members, and several areas that in the past was considered taboo. Yet in the past marriage between the races was also considered taboo. There does need to be tolerance for the choice people make about their lifestyle, but again it needs to not interfere with the beliefs and lifestyle of others.

Health care is simple enough. Americans hate the idea of national health care, but we need to rethink the idea. Insurance companies need to go away. The money needs to go directly into the health care system and the price of health care costs need to come down. The government needs to do incentives to help pay for medical school, change the malpractice system, and focus on just focus on direct health care without all of the extra costs. This means just one money payment comes out of our checks for health care period, not copays, no deductibles, and no extra charges or insurance premiums.

Poverty is a little harder. All Americans need access to higher education and vocational training in order to get into a good career. Children need to learn job skills in school not good grades. Impoverished neighborhoods need to be cleaned up and restored for people to live healthier, safer, and happier lives. The gap between the rich and the poor needs to be narrowed through education.

Children also need to be taught civility and tolerance towards others. The only way to overcome racism is through educating children about how there can be good in everyone and the best way to live life is to find ways to help others.

The federal government needs to be downsized and give more responsibilities to the states when it comes to domestic affairs. America does not need all of the security agencies it has. It is important for the federal government to make sure it can defend against other country, has a strong economy, excellent foreign affairs, and upholds the rights of the people through the constitution. If people's constitutional rights are being violated they need to be able to petition the federal government for help.

The federal government was able to step in and change segregation in the south and integrate schools. The federal government has also helped many people throughout the country to gain access to a better life through education and employment opportunities. It can continue to do these things.

The government also imprisoned thousands of Japanese Americans in internment camps during World War II. It also removed thousands of American Indians from their homes and put them on reservations. It has looked the other way when people have been oppressed, beaten, and killed over their religious beliefs.

In part it depends upon who is in power at the time. Those in power have the power to influence the country for good or evil. This is why it is so important to elect the right people for the job, and to become advocates for good in America and become involved in making a difference.

Chapter Three: Environment

"Those who contemplate the beauty of the earth find reserves of strength that will ensure as long as life lasts. There is something infinitely healing in the repeated refrains of nature - the assurance that dawn comes after night, and spring after winter."

Rachel Carson, Silent Spring

Silent Spring was published by Rachel Carson in 1962. It outlined what people were doing to the environment through the spraying of pesticides. The book had a lot of critics from big business and government officials. But none of them could deny the truth of what was going on. The book opened people's eyes to what was happening to the environment.

There were a lot of changes that took place to correct what was happening. America was able to reverse some of what it had done. There were other books and people throughout history who have championed the cause of helping to improve the environment.

The national park service and many other government land agencies help to preserve the land. States have made state parks to preserve areas within their borders that are not protected by the federal government. Cities have created green spaces with beautiful parks. Many countries around the world have followed the practice of preserving land through the establishment of national parks and animal reserves.

Yet despite the efforts of many well-meaning people there is still much of the land in danger or being destroyed. Many animals are at risk of becoming extinct. Rain forests are being cut down in alarming rates. In some areas of the world the land can no longer support the people that live there.

Climate Change

Climate change also referred to as global warming is real. Government officials and big business has tried to cover up and deny the facts for years. The fact is that no one can deny what is happening because of the changes that are taking place. Many scientists with a lot of evidence have concluded that the world is going through global warming which is creating a climate shift.

This means there will be a lot of changes taking place around the globe that will have a drastic impact on plants, animals, and people. The oceans will be rising which will cause many places like Bangladesh, the Netherlands, Venice, and Florida to become flooded.

There will be unbelievable storms more powerful than anyone has ever seen. Many of the animals of the earth will become extinct due to loss of habitat and the destructive forces of the storms. Some of the places on the earth will experience devastating droughts while others will experience floods. This will lead to a worldwide food shortage.

Forgotten Kingdoms

On Easter Island the inhabitants cut down most of the trees on the island and drastically impacted the environment. They have also introduced a rat that caused problems for plant life on the island. Many of the native animals became extinct including several birds. The population which was estimated to have been close to 15000 people dropped to only a few thousand by the time Europeans discovered the island. The inhabitants of the island may have resorted to cannibalism because of the lack of food.

The Kingdom of Kush or the Nubia was a wealthy kingdom that traded with its neighbors including Egypt. At one point Kush defeated Egypt and became very powerful. But there was widespread deforestation that took place which allowed the desert to take over many of the cities. The vast desert of the Sahara was not as big as it is today. The Sarah used to be an area filled with forests and animals. It eventually swallowed up the cities including those of the Kingdom of Kush.

Civilizations destroyed by Climate Change

Through history many civilizations have been destroyed due to a climate change. The Ancestral Puebloans built cities throughout the southwestern area of North America. These can still be seen at Mesa Verde and several other areas in the four corners region. Their civilization left after several years of drought due to a climate change.

The same thing happened to the Maya a once great civilization in central America that predates the Aztecs. The collapse of the Maya was brought on my a drought that lasted hundreds of years.

A major civilization in the Indus valley of India also collapsed due to a severe drought. The cities were actually built to capture as much of the rainfall as possible to help sustain its inhabitants and grow crops.

We do not know just how many civilizations were destroyed because of a climate change or environmental disaster. Scientists continue to find evidence of the collapse of several civilizations around the world that were severely impacted by different periods of climate change which resulted in droughts lasting several years or small ice-ages lasting several years.

The climate change we are experiencing will only get worse and may last hundreds of years if we do not do anything to stop the advancement of it. The damage to the environment can be reversed to some extent, but it will require a lot of effort worldwide.

Human Influence

The greatest debate over climate change for several decades has been if humans has caused it and if our actions are making it worse. If this is the case then there is something people can do to change the outcome. The Earth and its climates are very delicate and complicated, so to just say humans have cause this would be non-sense. The Earth does go through many different changes throughout history and in part it is going through one now. But it does look like humans have given the Earth a push in the global warming direction.

The problem is the green house gases that are in our atmosphere that trap the suns rays causing the temperature of the earth to raise. Just like when you get in a vehicle during a warm day. The vehicles is very hot, because the windows trapped the rays of the Sun causing the vehicle to become extremely hot. Venus is an example of a planet that has too much greenhouse gases. It is so hot on Venus that any spacecraft that lands on its surface will melt from the heat. There are many greenhouse gases, but it is carbon dioxide that seems to be the one that is increasing in alarming rates and will have the greatest impact on climate change.

Our carbon footprint or the amount of carbon we put into the atmosphere is what people focus on. This has led to people, cities, and governments to focus on renewable energy and sustainability. This means using energy from the Sun, wind, waves, and other creative means. The burning of fossil fuels releases the carbon into the atmosphere. Just think of all of the millions of cars on the road and coal factories producing electricity around the world. This would not be as bad if it wasn't for all of the trees being cut down. Trees being cut down will reduce the amount of carbon dioxide used by the trees and if trees are burned they release carbon into the atmosphere. The warming of the world will cause all of the carbon trapped in the tundra to be released when it is thawed.

Too much carbon is going into the atmosphere and not enough is being absorbed through plant life. The carbon once in the atmosphere will remain their for hundreds of years. So it is continually getting larger and larger.

A Wolf Story

In Europe people decided to get ride of all of the wolves because they did not want them to eat any of their livestock such as sheep and cattle. When Europeans came to America they brought with them their livestock and started to kill off the wolves. They felt like it was okay to exterminate the wolves. In their eyes they were even improving the environment. They thought that no predators was a good thing. This extermination even occurred in Yellowstone where forest rangers participated in the extermination of the wolves.

Several studies of Yellowstone showed that the absence of the wolves created an imbalance in the ecology of the region. Many animals without a natural predator became too numerous and thousands died from starvation in the winter like the elk. The plant and animal life of the park was greatly impacted. It mattered so much that there was a push to reintroduce the wolves.

It was through politics the wolves were exterminated from the park and it was through politics they came back. Today the wolves are still branded as an enemy by ranchers and hunters. Their days may be numbered determined by the politicians in office. The same thing is happening with environmental reforms today.

The Paris Agreement on climate change was a meeting where several countries around the world signed a document with the intent to help reduce the amount of fossil fuels used by the nations. 160 countries signed this including the United States. In June 2017 the United States announced they intended to withdraw from the agreement.

The problem is that the United States is one of the world's leading contributors of greenhouse gasses. If the United States does not follow through with its commitment to doing something with the environment it will be very difficult for anything to change to help improve our situation.

Call to Action

It is not just the federal governments of large countries that need to address environmental issues. Cities and rural communities need to find ways to be sustainable and rely more on renewable energy. People and families need to think about ways they can reduce their energy use and their carbon footprint.

The biggest challenge is to have big business and governments build infrastructures to accommodate changes that will enable people to be able to reduce or eliminate their carbon footprint. Driving an electric car and having solar panels on the roof of your house are good things to make an impact on people's carbon footprint.

Many people cannot afford to have solar panels and they do not get the great return promised. It often takes twenty years to start getting a return on your investment with solar panels and then it would be time to replace the ones you got. Sure you are doing your part for reducing the carbon in the atmosphere, but it is hard to do that when you are in debt. The price needs to come down and their needs to be more incentives by the government in the form of rebates and tax incentives. The electric companies need to find better ways to encourage people to go solar. The electric companies feel threatened by it and want to charge people with solar panels a lot of money just to be connected to the grid and make it so people cannot go off the grid. This is a form of totalitarianism that needs to be stopped through government regulation if necessary.

One of the biggest issues is changing the energy we receive from coal to renewables. Electric companies need to replace their coal power plants with energy from the sun, wind, water, and thermal sources. It will cost a lot of money in the short term, but if there is government incentives involved and the companies take the plunge it could work. Even nuclear energy would be a safer alternative to coal. The electric companies would do so much better in the long term. If they do not take action soon they will end up losing a lot of money, because the people will demand their change and eventually they will have to be taken over by someone else.

Electric vehicles are a great idea. They have been around for about 100 years only the technology is finally starting to get caught up with gas vehicles. They now can go faster and further than before. But the infrastructure is still not there yet. You cannot go on a road trip with an electric car to many areas, because there is no place to recharge your car. Then there is also the waiting for your car to charge. So if you want to wait around for 30 minutes with a rapid charge station you are set. Plus you would have to do this every 100 miles. One a road trip even with charging stations along the way an electric car can add several more hours. The batteries in an electric car last a few hundred thousand miles and then you have to buy new ones which are in the thousands. This makes electric cars very expensive and not practical unless your commute to work is less than 50 miles roundtrip.

Many countries in Europe have put in place an infrastructure for electric cars and have given enough incentives to help people afford them. Things will not change until the industry and the government gets together to make a difference.

Plus getting an electric car does not reduce your carbon footprint if the electricity you are using to charge your car comes from a coal burning plant. In other words everyone could own electric cars and there can still be a problem with global warming if there are still coal burning plants charging those cars.

The other thing people needs to do especially Americans is to reduce the amount of energy we are consuming. We use more energy per person than most countries in the world. This puts a lot of effort into running coal burning power plants and maintaining a high level of energy to support the amount of energy used by the people. The growing population of the United States means there will be a greater need for more energy, which could result in the building of more coal power plants and more carbon put into the atmosphere.

New homes need to be built with energy conservation in mind. Gone should be the houses built fast and without energy conservation in mind. Houses should be able to stay cool in the summer and warm in the winter with minimal energy consumption. This means thicker walls, less wasted place, thicker windows, and more ambient lighting. We need more architects to get with contractors to build these types of homes. Many of the new homes built are large and beautiful, but require a lot of energy to maintain a comfortable temperature. In the long run the homes end up costing the homeowner a lot more in utilities bills than they can afford. People need to start settling for smaller homes that are more energy efficient.

We cannot wait for others to start doing things about the environment. We can reduce energy costs in our homes and drive energy efficient vehicles that have low emissions. If you live close to work you may want to start to think about riding a bike. If public transportation works of you then start using it. Individuals and families can start to do little things to make a difference.

Cities all around the world are starting to do a lot of things to help reduce their carbon footprint. Many of them are putting in bike paths, developing public transportation using renewable energy, building renewable energy plants, and creating green spaces.

People are given incentives to drive electric cars and install solar panels for their homes.

There will come a time when things will be reversed and it will be cheaper to go green than to continue to use fossil fuels. Countries that rely on fossil fuels for income will go bankrupt overnight. Automobile companies that do not develop new technology for vehicles that use renewable energy will go out of business.

Chapter Four: Education

"Education is not preparation for life; education is life itself."

John Dewey

According to a US News report for rankings of education in countries. Canada was ranked number one, the United Kingdom was number two, Germany was number three, Australia was number four, France was number five, Switzerland was number six, and the United States was number seven. Education is often evaluated on test proficiency of students. Some of the countries in the top five manage their educational system differently than the United States. In Germany and in the UK students are placed in tracks and given vocational education to get into a career.

The United States does a good job of following a factory model and educating all children from age five through 16. It is because of the diversity of the students and the lack of focusing on the students many students fall behind in mastering skills and end up dropping out of high school. It is those in poor social economic classes and English language learners that have the hardest time keeping up with their classes. There are several state and federal programs that attempt to compensate for educational gap these students are facing, but this does not enough to help all of these children.

The United States is facing a crisis of a generation that does not have the skills necessary for 21st century jobs. Many of these jobs will be going to people from other countries. The gap between the poor and wealthy will be getting larger as children drop out of school and attempt to live off of minimum paying jobs. Many children even those who do graduate from high school and college will lack the skills necessary to be successful in their chosen career and in the most basic of relationships. The people who will be the CEOs and owners of businesses will be foreign nationals. Children will not be able to communicate with other people around the world to do business. They will not have the skills to solve problems or work cooperatively with others.

The United States is fixated on the factory model where students come in sit in a row and listen to the teacher while they take notes and then study to pass a test. This reaches the masses who come to public schools, but it does little in teaching essential skills students need to succeed in life. Schools have come along way and there are many schools focusing on what they call, "Best practices." There are a number of programs schools and districts implement in an attempt to improve education. Many of them are positive and help students, but these programs do not often address major school challenges and only focus on a handful of students.

Grade Level

The first issue with public education in the United States is age based grade levels. A child turns a certain age and is placed in a grade level with other children the same age. There are standards and even reading assessments based on what is appropriate for the age of a child. This is ridiculous, because children are at different levels of development and skills.

There are children far advanced than their peers yet they are not allowed to move up to the next grade. Then there are children who are very immature and lack skills that are continually advanced with other children the same age. This creates a number of challenges such as children being bored with work they are not challenged with. Children acting up because they are not able to do the work. Then there is also children that are unable to coop with children their own age, or do not have the social maturity to be in an upper level class. All of these challenges are placed on the school and the teachers resulting in less learning taking place and fewer students able to master essential skills in the most basic of classes.

It makes sense that grade level should be based on skill not age. Students who master skills are moved up in grade level and those who struggle are kept back until they master the skills. This should also be the case with social maturity. So that by the time children reach high school they are ready to learn what they need to enter college or start to prepare for a career.

Many students would be more motivated if they knew they could move up, and motivated to move up so they would not be left behind. This would allow many students to excel at a greater rate than before, and it would allow teachers to be able to challenge students with more rigor in the classroom and focus on the skills instead of just coming up with filler activities or busy work to fill the time for the rest of a term. Teachers would find that they would have a greater impact on students and enjoy their jobs a lot more.

Assessments

We are a test taking people. In many of the industrialized countries of the world students are expected to take tests. These are often high stake tests that determine which college a student will attend and what career she can go into. Yet the tests in themselves do not really test the skills students have mastered, the social ability to connect with others, and the ability of students to be hard workers, or just how fair they are in their dealings with others.

There is a place in education for assessments. They can check the understanding of students and determine the progress students are making. The assessments need to be a true test of a student's ability and mastery of a skill. Assessments should not be paper and pencil tests, or even the tests now taken on the computer. There is a possibility of making computer simulations that will test a students ability. These are often done with pilots. Yet there is still nothing compared to the real thing.

A pilot is not going to receive his license on simulations alone. He needs to get in a plane and fly it to determine his skills. It is only through hours of flying that he is able to be able to become a skilled pilot people can trust with their lives.

The same thing is true about driving a car. Virtually all students go through drivers education and are taken on the road where they have to spend several hours behind the wheel driving. Then when they are ready to take their drivers test there is both a driving and written test.

In order to graduate from high school students only need to pass their classes and take a couple of tests. The are not assessed on essential abilities they may need for success like communication skills, technology skills, and problem solving skills. Just think how different high school graduation would be if all students had to go through a series of hands on problem solving activities that really challenged their abilities.

Throughout history children have been challenged enough to develop survival skills in order to be able to live to become an adult and raise the next generation. Many children did not get a formal education. They learned the skills to become a farmer, to hunt, to build a home, and to work with others to get things done.

In the period of the world wars people had to develop the skills to fight, to work hard to provide for their families, to figure out ways to survive the shortages everyone faced. Children learned to be frugal during the Great Depression of the thirties and to reuse items in their homes.

Today in America children do not face the threat of being drafted to go to war, they do not know the challenges people faced during the Great Depression, and do not understand what challenges they will have to face as they become adults.

Suicide has increased significantly in the past decade in part because of poverty and a higher divorce rate. Many children become at risk because they feel less confident about their abilities and are not taught valuable skills to coop with the challenges they face in their lives. When they graduate from high school they do not have the skills to be able to deal with not being able to get a job to support their family, or do not have the social skills to maintain healthy relationships.

Children often become discouraged when they fail high stake tests. These tests are based on a particular group of people, and they can be extremely difficult for some children to be able to pass despite the skills they have mastered and their ability to do other things. A test will not determine the ability of a student to do work in college or what kind of worker she might. High stake tests have been proven to place a great deal of stress on students causing depression and suicidal thoughts.

Subjects Taught

Who determines what is taught in school? Most schools fall under a school board that makes the decision which reflects the state requirements. People in the state government and school boards who by the way may have no educational background make the decisions for what is taught and required in the schools. This is often driven by people who think a certain subject area is really important.

The honest truth of the matter is most subjects are have important things for children to know. The problem really isn't the subjects being taught it is how the subjects are represented at the school. Traditionally students have English (language arts), history (social studies), science, and math that are required each day. Then comes physical education, health, and technology classes that are only required for part of the time. Last of all students are required to take some elective courses that often fall into a fine arts or performing arts class. Most schools also offer language classes like Spanish and German. Then there are some specialty classes like shop and computer programing.

The difficulty is that a class may not be offered in one school, but offered in another. One school might offer French and Chinese, but other schools don't. Children who want to take these classes would have to transfer to this school which could be very difficult to do and require a parent to drive her child to school everyday. There are charter and private schools that specialize in certain areas. Some public school may have a certain program while other school do not offer the program. Some schools have a more successful program than another school. This can be reflected in sports and performing arts programs.

This means that many children roll the dice when it comes to learning things they want to learn in the schools they are going to. Many schools don't even advertise the programs they offer. Students are only able to determine what kind of programs they have by attending the school and then if they are not satisfied with the program is becomes a nightmare to attempt to transfer to another school with the program they want to enter into.

Children often end up with a schedule heavy on the required classes and very light on the elective classes with very few options with electives. No wonder many children do not like school and become frustrated attending. Those who came up with the requirement may argue students just need to focus on passing their required classes and just take the elective classes that may help them get into college. Many colleges require certain things like several years of a foreign language or classes in technology.

The hard part with subjects taught is being able to match up the classes with the interests of the students and to be able to maximize their schedule to help students met the requirements for college and to be able to qualify for scholarships. The dilemma is that one student becomes overwhelmed with all of the AP or honors classes she is taking and ends up having a nervous breakdown, and the other students becomes bored with school due to the lack of interest in his classes.

States and school boards need to come up with creative ways to help motivate students to stay in school. This means they reduce the number of required classes and increase the number of elective classes with an emphasis on career building skills. Required classes like math, science, and technology can be integrated into one STEM class. History, language arts, and fine arts can be combined. Physical Education and health can be combined. Then students can spend the rest of their time taking classes they really want to take becoming excited about coming to school and learning.

Schools can be creative in the classes they offer students by combining classes and creating online classes for students to take while they are at home and on break. There are so many opportunities for students to take the classes they want to take instead of just taking the ones they are required to take.

The grades issued by teachers is also a detriment to the students. What determines a letter grade in the class? Does the same letter grade mean the same in a different school or a different state? An "A" in one class may require a lot more effort in one class than in another. If a student received a letter grade of a "D" he will receive the credit for the class, but it basically says that the student made an effort in class to pass, but does not know the material and hasn't mastered the skills.

Call to Action

Standardized testing and high stake testing needs to be thrown out. There is no place in education for such non-sense. Especially when the students are not held accountable for the testing and it is only used to measure the growth of the student to grade the school and not as a benchmark for students to determine skill master to move into a different grade.

The grades assigned to students in classes needs to be changed to "M" for mastery or "N" for not mastered. Students with a "M" move on to another class and those with a "N" remain to be able to reach mastery. This makes the grading process easier and students know what they need to do in order to pass the class and master the skills. Teachers learn how to recognize what it takes to help students master skills.

Students should be able to have the ability to move up grade levels as they master skills. Students should also be able to remain behind in order to work on mastering skills and then move up after the skills are mastered.

Students also should be able to with the help of parents and counselors choose the path they take through school taking the elective classes they want to take and not having to be overloaded with required classes. The required classes need to be integrated, hands on, and career based.

Chapter Five: Economy

"Rather go to bed without dinner than to rise in debt."

Benjamin Franklin

Many nations and people around the world are fixated on being in debt. The philosophy is that debt is the modern way of being economically sound. This deficit spending concept is not very new, in fact it was introduced before the Great Depression. Part of the cause of the depression was that many people borrowed money or went into debt to buy stocks and then when the stocks became worthless not only did they lose their money, but they owed banks the money they borrowed for the stocks. People could not pay the banks back so the banks went bankrupt.

In the housing crisis of 2008 the same thing happened. People bought houses they could not afford. Their mortgage was sold and resold to different financial groups and those financial institutions were stuck with the mortgage and lost a lot of money.

The government has been spending money going trillions of dollars in debt and continues to have a policy of deficit spending. The idea is that when the economy is not where it needs to be the government spends money to stimulate the economy to bring it back up. This has been going on for decades and the government gets involved with spending a lot of money for the military. The United States spends more for its military than Russia and China combined. It would be great if this was really working and the economy was constantly stalemated by deficit spending.

The reality is that there will be a point when the United States is so far in debt that it will not be able to pay its loans and it will default on the loans causing the dollar to go way down in value hurting the inflation in the United States. It could set off a chain reaction bringing a lot of financial institutions and people down with many people losing their money and not being able to pay for debts.

The inflation in Germany during the 1920's following World War I was out of control. The mark became worthless causing Germany to sink into a severe depression. It also created an atmosphere of fear and desperation. Hitler and his Nazi party was able to gain the necessary votes to get into power. The economic crisis set the stage for Germans to blame the Jews for their misfortune allowing for the Holocaust to happen.

Debt and Interest

Banks make money by charging interest for the loans they give to people. Credit card companies also make money charging interest for the charges people make on items. The interest allows many people to make money through investments. People can make money by being pain interest through savings accounts and various certificates. It is a delicate circle of debt and interest that goes around the world.

Money in the bank goes to build someone's home, it may be put into stocks and bond, or it may go to pay for a vehicle. Money does not just sit idly by and do nothing unless it is in someone's desk drawer at home or under the mattress.

The problem comes when there is a break in the circle. A person is unable to pay the interest on the loan they borrowed. This break causes a ripple effect where the bank may lose money and has to pay less interest to those with a savings account. The ripple effect may extent to the government that will cover the loan of banks that cannot make the payment. Basically what happens is that the ripple effect has an impact on the economy.

People with less money are not able to shop at businesses. The businesses close their doors and let go their employees. The employees are unable to pay their bills and the banks are hit with the money and have to shut down. Thus unemployment goes up, people are without money, and inflation starts to run out of control. Chaos and pandemonium rages through the streets and their is despair and fear in the faces of those walking the streets looking for soup kitchens or handouts.

Everything is okay if their is not a break in the economic circle of debt and interest. If the interest is being paid things are okay. What happens is that people and businesses take upon too much debt and are unable to pay the interest. If you are living beyond your means meaning you are unable to pay your bills and the interest you owe on your debts you will start to lose things like your home and cars.

It is far easier to get a loan and credit cards than in the past. People can go into debt faster and deeper than anytime before. They become slaves to the interest they owe. If you are not making any progress in paying down your debts then you are a slave to those debts until you can pay them off. You have less financial freedom if all of the money you make goes just to paying off interest.

The key when it comes to debt and interest is to be debt free and earn interest through investments, certificates, and savings accounts. There are some who would argue a little debt is healthy and the government needs to continue with deficit spending in order for us to not go into a recession. Then there are others who argue for a balanced budget and not going into debt.

The safe bet would be to have a balanced budget both in the country and at home. The risk would be to go into debt in order to be able to make more money or have something you do not have. You may want a home so you get a loan for it. This is okay if you can pay the interest and be on your way to pay down the loan and still have enough to be able to buy food and pay your other bills and even have enough left over to put into savings or invest with.

If you go into debt and do not have enough money to do the other things you will start to dig a deeper whole of debt you may not be able to recover from. It may reach the point you have to default on your loans and lose your home and many of your possessions.

The same holds true with the government. The deeper it goes into the debt the more it will impact the money it has to pay out. This means government employees will be impacted. The grants that go to education and other organizations will be impacted. Each year the president and congress agree upon a budget for the next year. If they see the are in the red, they will start thinking about many programs to cut. Yet if they see that they have extra money in the budget they will be more generous to programs that are requesting more money.

There are times when the country may need to spend extra money to help boost the economy, and there are times when people need to take out a loan. But common sense suggests that at these times the country and people need to make certain they have enough money to be able to survive on before going into debt. Just think about how great it would be if the country was out of debt and had some extra money to invest or play around with. Think about how wonderful it would be if other countries came to the United States for loans instead of the United States taking out loans.

Think about times in your life when you didn't have the burden of debt hanging over your head. How did you feel? Think of a time when you had some extra money. It feels great looking at a bank statement and seeing extra money you have in your savings account. It is hard for parents to pay for their children's education if they have no money. It is hard to be able to pay for celebrations like birthdays and weddings without having some money. There are some countries where the parents have to go into debt to pay for the wedding of their daughter and it takes then several years to pay off the debt.

There was a time when there was no money and people survived through trading or just simply providing a service or produce to the village. There would be someone who made shoes for everyone in the village and in return he would get food from neighbors who specialized in dairy products, baked breads, and vegetables. Maybe we someday will return to this idea state of economy.

Call to Action

You need to do all you can to get debt free and remain debt free. Pay off your credit cards every month. The only two loans you should ever have are home and vehicle loans. You need a place to live and need transportation to work. If you can live without a car great. Cars cost a lot of money in insurance, registration, and maintenance. If you do get a vehicle get something that you can afford and something that is practical. I have never owned a large SUV or truck because I have never had a need for them. If I was to buy a large SUV or truck I would have had to pay a lot more in insurance and overall expenses not to mention the initial price of the vehicle in the first place. The same holds true with sports cars and luxury cars. Common sense tells me that I should buy cars that hold their value, are reliable, and work well for where I live.

Homes are the same as vehicles. You do not want to buy a home you cannot afford. You also do not want to buy a home that is not practical for your needs. If you have a large family and have your extended family living with you a large house would be more practical. But if you have a small family and have no need for a large home do not buy one. The things you should be looking for in a home is the location and what you might need in a home.

Location is so important because you want to be able to get along with your neighbors, feel safe, and enjoy where you live. You want to be close to where you work and close enough to schools and other places you frequent. You may want to live in a place with a nice view as well. The location will also impact the value of the home. In a good location the value of your home will increase.

The United States government is way to large. There needs to be a huge downsizing of all of its agencies. The state governments should be allowed to focus more on the domestic issues and the federal government the foreign issues.

The amount spend on the military needs to come down. America spends way too much on the military. It is important America is able to defend itself and to be able to have the power to bring about a positive influence in the world, but this can be done without having to spend so much.

Income tax needs to be either done with a set tax where employers take out so much and there is no need to file taxes every year, or income tax needs to be removed entirely. Either way it would be good for the economy.

A fixed tax would enable the government to be able to collect more taxes, it would be fair across the board, and people would not have to stress out every year trying to file their taxes. Many Americans would be willing to pay a little more in taxes if they knew they didn't have to file taxes anymore. There would not longer be a need for the IRS to hire as many people to help out with taxes each year.

Doing away with the income tax would give people more money to invest with, put into retirement, and to buy things that would stimulate the economy. People would have more money in their pockets which is always a better thing for the economy. The government would actually save money, because it would not have to go into deficit spending attempting to stimulate the economy. Originally there was no income tax until the Revenue Act of 1861 which was passed to pay for the Civil War. It was repealed ten years later. Then the 16th amendment was ratified in 1913 that brought about income tax. The idea of income tax was not popular among conservatives at the time and for many people today they would jump for joy if they didn't have to pay income tax anymore.

The Social Security Act was signed into law by President Roosevelt in 1935 which gives income to people at a certain age that seems to keep rising. The money taken out of our paychecks goes to support the people who have retired. It is also suppose to support us when we retire, but there may not be any money in the system when many people do finally retire. It is a program that has well meaning ideas, but is poorly managed. It could be far better if people were allowed to put the money into their own retirement and choose to opt out of social security. Ministers do have this option, but they need to make sure they are covered for retirement, because they will not receive any social security benefits if they opt out.

The government needs to be thinking of more ways to put money back into people's pockets and not be taking it away. The same goes with the amount of money spent on health care. If we only had to pay a fixed percentage of our income on health care it would save people a lot of money and stress over health care costs.

Chapter Six: Family

"Our children need strong families raising them with sturdy virtues, not to be smothered in the cold arms of the state."

Margaret Thatcher

The family is the single most important element of a strong country. Without families country become weak and start to deteriorate. Years of research tell us that children are more successful in a stable family structure than children who are raised in a broken family where there is one or more parents absent and the family atmosphere is one of abuse or neglect. It is common sense families are the best places to teach children to be successful, to be good citizens, and to learn virtues that will help them contribute to society.

Today the family is under attack. There are more children being born outside of wedlock, the divorce rate continues to climb, and many couples chose not to get married at all. Families less stable as they were in the past, and some people take family responsibilities lightly especially men who leave their families, are absent fathers, or who enter into a relationship without taking on the responsibility of caring for the children.

It is the children who suffer the most when a family has fallen apart. Some children never experience belonging to a solid family and drift with a single parent who has multiple relationships and moves several times going from one job to the next. Then there are the children who are moved from one foster family to the next. There are parents who are unfit to raise children, because of drug abuse, immaturity, and stressful situations. Children grow up not knowing what a traditional family is like and when they start to have children they raise them like what they experienced when they were a child. The lack of family support becomes a viscous cycle that is hard to break.

Marriage

The family starts with marriage, which is a commitment between two people. It is a responsibility to take care of each other, respect each other, and to support each other in all of the challenging situations that may come throughout life. It becomes a legal responsibility to each other as well as a spiritual bound that transforms any other relationship. This is the ideal when it comes to marriage.

In such a marriage where the couple works together in harmony to make a life together wonderful things happen. There is an enormous about of joy and happiness that comes with such a marriage. They are able to accomplish things they couldn't dream of before getting married. They are able to support each other when one is going through a tough time. They are there for each other.

The pain of loneliness and despair leave as a married couple bonds with each other. They become best friends who work, play, and care for each other. There is no person or thing that can tear them apart. The devotion they have for each other is unbreakable and endless.

This is what happens in a perfect marriage. A marriage where miracles happen. A marriage where the rewards are unlimited. Such a marriage creates the ideal family where both parents support each other in becoming the best parents they can be. They raise children to be good people and productive citizens. They raise their children to get married and start the process over again.

In a community where there are these types of marriages there is no poverty, no crime, no challenges that are too great. The problems of society are taken care of through the right marriage and the raising of children in such a marriage.

The reality of it is that marriage is tough. Couples disagree on things. People have bad habits that drive their spouse crazy. It can be extremely hard to live with someone 24/7. You may first experience this with a roommate in college.

It can be really hard to find the right person to take the plunge with. You may try to find someone who is perfect, who has the same interests as you, the same values, and the same background as you. No one who is perfect and even a person who shares the same interests and has the same background can turn out to be a big jerk. Everyone has flaws, weaknesses, and makes mistakes from time to time.

The challenges in society when it comes to marriage is the lack of responsibility, commitment, and true love involved in the process. It seems like people jump into a relationship because they are attracted to each other and allow their physical relationship guide their decisions. Then when they get married they find out they really do not like each other all that much and get a divorce. People get married without getting to know the other person and find out they don't like many of the things the other person does. There are some who get married young and have a hard time as one person matures and the other doesn't, or both lack the maturity to deal with serious issues marriage involves.

The ideas of relationships are often represented in stories, the media, and movies. We see movie stars having romantic relationships with several people lacking the devotion to one person. Society tells us that it is okay to test drive a relationship and not commit to marriage. It is okay to not take marriage too serious, because you can always get a divorce and find someone else. Love is based on lust and the physical relationship, not a unconditional act of devotion to each other.

Fifty percent of divorces end in divorce. This is an extremely high percentage of failed marriages. It also means that half of families become broken. People look at this rate and decide they will just not get married. The problem with this type of thinking is that they have an even higher rate of not being committed to one person. They tend to go from on partner to another without really having the commitment that can take place in marriage.

In the past it was taboo to get a divorce even when there was severe abuse going on in the marriage. Marriage were also arranged by parents or a matchmaker and couples may have not even seen each other until their wedding day. Yet somehow this worked. Couples learned to love each other and knew they were stuck with each other until death. It was not good for those who went through the abuse or had to live with someone they despised. It did work for those who understood marriage meant you are devoted to your spouse.

Parenthood

Parenthood starts with having a good marriage. Couples that are committed to each other often make good parents, because they are willing to share the responsibility of raising a child and learn together to be good parents. Couples that fight often and are not compatible with each other will often make poor parents. It is a matter of commitment, dedication, patience, and unconditional love.

Any parent would agree they are not perfect and the first attempt at being a parent there are a not of mistakes made. Some people are better at being parents than others. It is a matter of being prepared and being responsible for the welfare and teaching of the child.

A parent cannot just feed, clothes, and provide a roof over the child's head. A parent needs to show love to the child through acts of kindness. A parent should help the child deal with challenges such as learning to tie shoes, ride a bike, and attend school. A parent needs to be there for a child and spend quality time with the child. A parent needs to be a role model for the child showing kindness for others, being patient with people, and being humble about making mistakes. Being a parent is the single most important role on the planet with an enormous responsibility. It is more important than the president of the United States, the Catholic Pope, and being the richest person in the world. A parent can have greater influence on a child than anyone.

Just like marriage society and the media tells us that it is okay not to be a responsible parent. It is okay to leave your child when they are young and have no contact with them. It is okay to have several children with different people.

Today children may not go through as much physical abuse as in the past. But they go through a lot of neglect. It might not be neglect in the form of not having enough food, it comes in the form of not having a parent around when the child needs one. The neglect comes when the child doesn't have anyone to talk to about her troubles at school, or someone to tell she scored a goal at her game. Parents even those who are considered good parents will find themselves too busy to get involved with their child's life. Both parents will work long hours and be caught up with the busy things of life and will forget how precious the time is while spending it with their children.

Parenthood is harder than marriage. It requires a lifelong commitment to someone who needs a lot of help early on in life to get started. It requires a lot of patience, sacrifice, and heartache. You may find that even after all of the time and effort you devote to your children they will make some terrible mistakes that will break your heart. But it becomes all worth it when they come back to you and seek your advice on how to raise their own children and you are able to see how wonderful your grandchildren are.

There is a trend of parents wanting to give up the power of being a parent and just being friends with their children. They have a fear of losing their children so they try to act like their children and allow their children a lot of freedom to do what they want to do. There is a lack of discipline in this type of parenting and the children will display lack of respect for their parents.

Children

One of the ten commandments says to obey your parents. There have been laws where children who do not obey their parents were killed. It does say in the bible that a child that does not obey his parents must be taken and stoned. We are not so drastic today with misbehaving children. In some ways we have swung to the opposite site of the spectrum. Children will sometimes rule the family doing as they please while the parents out of frustration and fear sit idly by as the family sinks into chaos.

In many cultures of the world parents are respected. Children obey their parents, because it is part of their way of life. It is not just the parents that are shown respect, it is any adult. The language has a built in way of showing respect how you speak to someone.

America does not have such cultural traditions when it comes to respect for adults or parents. In the past their was an expectation children would show respect, but today this expectation is only observed by a few communities and is often passed on in the families not the community. Religious groups may also place an emphasis on showing respect for adults and obeying parents.

The trend is to be cool with people. This is displayed by how children dress, act, and speak to others. Adults are no longer addressed with polite titles but with first names or ignorant slang titles. The handshake has been replaced by the fist bump or some sort of strange hand signal.

Children are spending more time with friends than they are at home with their families. They are becoming more influenced by their peers than they do by their parents. This is not all that bad unless the children are spending time with friends that are doing bad things and friends that are abusive.

Children turn their attention to their peers and feel more empowered by the opinion of their peers than they do their parents. They will see what their friends are doing and want to act the way their friends act about their parents. This is also influenced by the movies or television they see. Gone are the days of, "Father knows Best, and Leave it to Beaver." Now children have shows where the children disobey their parents and it is portrayed as being funny or really cool.

It is hard enough to raise children today. It is nearly impossible to do it without a strong family support. There are just too many challenges children have to face these days. We need to give children a heads start on their future with them being raised in a strong family.

Call to Action

Marriage needs to be looked at a sacred covenant two people have with each other. Married couples need to take seriously their marriage and be devoted to each other without the idea that it is okay to get a divorce or to step out with someone else. There needs to be fidelity within marriage and harmony among spouses. If a couple is not willing to take on such a commitment to each other they should just remain friends and look for someone else who can be committed to them.

States should require couple to go through a marriage class before receiving a marriage license and continue to receive counseling for the first year after marriage. This is vital to help ensure healthy marriages that will spark good families. Just think about it, we would not argue that everyone should go through drivers education and take a test in order to get a drivers license. Why do we take something as precious and important as marriage and make it so trivial?

Married couples that want to have children should go through a parenting class and continue to have evaluations through the first year of being a parent. It is interesting how society values human life. A fetus has zero rights and infant has only a few, and children until they are considered an adult still doesn't have many rights. We allow everyone to have a child weather their fit to raise a child or not. It isn't until a child has been abused for several years or has a fatal accident that the government starts to take notice.

If all parents had to register as parents and go through training as well as being monitored for the first year of a child's life we would be able to deal with a lot of neglect and abuse that takes place in families. If this happened couples would take upon more responsibility for having children.

Parents who cannot demonstrate support and commitment to their child should not be allowed to raise the child. The foster program needs to be strict on their guidelines with foster parents. The program should also give children in the program financial support for college.

There should be youth facilities throughout the country that are specifically for troubled youth that parents are unable to control. These programs should work with parents and children to come up with solutions so that parents feel they have more control in working with their children, and a place they can send their child that is being disobedient. This allows parents an alternative that prevents abuse and ends up waking up the child to his situation.

Chapter Seven: Religion

"A through knowledge of the Bible is worth more than a college education."

Theodore Roosevelt

Some would say we do not need religion anymore. The number of people who belong to a religion has decreased in many industrialized countries. Even those who say they belong to a religion they seldom attend church and do not follow the basic practices of their religion. There are those who may even attack religion saying that it causes hate, bigotry, and violence. This of course refers to the opposition between different religious groups over simply choosing to have a different lifestyle than each other.

There have been the holy wars of the past where Christians went in and fought against Muslims during the crusades of the middle ages. Christians were attempting to retake Jerusalem from the Muslims. The Muslims had for years fought against other religions in order to gain advantage of territory and power. Throughout history different sects of each religion fought each other because of different opinions. The Catholics of Northern Ireland and the protestants of England fought for decades to gain power in Northern Ireland. Sunni and Shia muslims have fought for hundreds of years to gain power in Iraq and Iran.

Today regardless of religion there are Muslims fighting Muslims, and Christians fighting Christians. Every once in a while a group attempts genocide in a region to get ride of Jews or Muslims or Christians. So there a few who argue religion is a bad thing because of the conflict between religions.

The truth is that it doesn't matter if they are fighting in under the pretense they doing in the name of God, it is not correct. They are fighting just to gain an upper hand of where they live. They want the power of the region and want to be able to control the people. This is hard to do unless they can get rid of those people who are different than they are.

There is an argument for science that says God does not exist because we cannot prove he exists. Religionists would argue people need to have faith in order to believe God exists. Then there is a third group that believes science and religion can coexist. They believe religion and science go hand in hand together. Many religious leaders believe in scientific theories including the theory of evolution. Many scientific leaders also believe in religion.

The majority of the population in the world have some religious beliefs, but do not activity participate in a religion or believe religion in general is necessary. This argument is that it is okay to live a religious life being a good person without having to belong to a religion or participate in religious services. They make up their own form of worship and way of being religious without going to a church.

Fanaticism

The violence and intolerance in the world that is done in the name of God is done through a fanatical religious zealots. They believe they are right and everyone else is wrong. They alter the words in sacred text to fit their agenda. These people are in the minority, but often get the most attention. They promote evil and create in the minds of people a stereotype that all people who belong to this religion are the same way.

An example of this is Islamic terrorists that claim they are committing murder in the name of God. The both are brainwashed and brainwash other recruits into thinking what they are doing is the will of God. In reality they are following their own agenda and have a narrow point of view the they are doing the right thing and everyone else is doing the wrong thing. They are judging everyone else, and not taking a look at what they are doing. They are not just targeting Americans, Europeans, Christians, or other Muslims that are part of a different sect. They are killing Muslims that are of the same sect that just do not believe in the same exact agenda as they do.

They have strange beliefs that have nothing to do with Islam like the oppression of women and the strict code of conduct they feel everyone should follow like not listening to music. The Taliban was a classic example of this how they put the people of Afghanistan in a sort of martial law where people were forbidden to do many of the traditions like celebrate a marriage.

The same fanaticism is found in just about all religions including Christianity. There are Christians who have killed other Christians because they were doing something they felt was wrong. Throughout Europe countries ruled through church law according to the interpretation of that law by local clergy resulting in many people being burned at the stake.

In America there has been many cases of religious intolerance where people were killed and banished from area. Anne Hutchinson was banished from her community when she held Bible lessons out of her home. The local religious leaders who were men felt threatened by her authority and wanted to get rid of her. The governor of Missouri issued an extermination order to kill or drive Mormons from the state in 1838. Many Mormons were forced from their homes and killed. Most were able to flee to nearby Illinois where about ten years later were forced from that state as well.

The Need for Religion

Religion is not evil it is those who use it for gain and power that are evil. It is the fanaticism that is evil and the religious zealots that cause the problems. There are a lot of good people in the world both religious and non-religious. It is important to distinguish the stereotypes and half-truths about a religion.

The world without religion was filled with chaos and violence. People had no sense of direction or purpose. The Hebrews went from being in slavery with the Egyptians to being led out of Egypt by Moses who received the Ten Commandments from God. The Ten Commandments helped the Hebrews become an organized powerful people because of the focus on those laws. Even today many people follow the Ten Commandments and their laws are based on them.

The Jewish people have survived thousands of years of oppression and exile because of the traditions of their religion. It is what gives them a sense of identity and purpose.

Religion gives hope to billions of people who seek relief from their pain and sorrows. People worship to find peace from the challenges they face each day. It is what drives a lot of people to become successful and to do amazing things in their lives.

The amount of charity alone that is driven by religion is staggering. In many parts of the world it is the sacrifice given by religions and their followers that help to keep people alive, bring them out of poverty, and give aid in times of crisis. When there is a disaster or global emergency it is the religions that come together to be the first to give aid to the victims. Pure religion teaches people to give alms to the poor, help those in need, and seek to do good in the world. If it wasn't for religion the call for help would go unanswered.

Sacred texts like the Bible, Quran, and Book of Mormon are valuable spiritual teachers to humanity. They ground a person's beliefs and help them to become more tolerant and forgiving of others. These books are not only classics that all children should read they are the foundation of a better society. Just think about what today would be if there was no Bible. The messages Jesus Christ gave in the New Testament are priceless as well as the teachings of the Buddha. These messages have transformed the world into a better one and will continue to transform the hearts of people for centuries to come.

Church and State

The first amendment of the Constitution of the Untied States states; "Congress shall make no law respecting an establishment of religion, or prohibiting the free exercise thereof; ..." This is known as separation of church and state and freedom of religion in America.

There is a misconception among people that everything religious needs to be done away with and the founding fathers were not religious and didn't want religion in the country. The opposite is true the founding fathers were very religiously minded and believed the freedom of religion in America was very important. They believe that it was important to be tolerant of religion and not to have one religion dominate another or control the government. This brought about the idea of separation of both government and religious powers. In other words one particular religion should not be allowed to make laws for everyone else, but that the religion and those who practice the religion can practice it without interference from the government.

One example of church and state involves education. Almost all the schools for hundreds of years had strong religious ties. Many children learned to read by reading the Bible in school. It wasn't until the 1960s and 70s that school districts started to remove everything religious from schools. Daily prayer used to be apart of school and now it is not. The study of the Bible was common and now it is only read as a literature piece.

The strange thing is that schools across the country still celebrate religious holidays like Christmas, Halloween, and Easter. There is nothing wrong with having religion in schools, the problem is only promoting one religion and forcing the children to do religious activities.

Children can learn a lot by the study of many different religions. It first teaches them tolerance for other cultures, and helps them to appreciate what other people believe. Children are able to be friends with other children who are from a different church than they are. It would be impossible to teach geography or history without including the study of religion. The study of religion is essential to stop children from being intolerance and prejudice towards other children of other faiths. Ignorance is the seed of hate.

Call to Action

We must ensure that religious freedom continues in the United States and we seek religious freedom for people all around the world. It is only through religious freedom and the diversity of religious thought that people can live in harmony with each other. Laws need to be reinforced to protect religious freedom.

Schools need to teach about religion and religious tolerance. Children need to read the Bible and other sacred texts to learn about the foundation of other religions and the origins of civilizations. Children need to be taught the differences between religion and how religious thought has influenced cultures around the world.

Chapter Eight: Voice of Hope

My first thoughts about writing this book was to write about all of the bad things happening in the world and some suggestions in fixing them. The title was going to be a Voice of Warning, but the more I thought about it, the more I did not like it. My intent is not to write about how awful the world is right now, my intent is to give the world a wake up call to what is happening and to say we still have time to fix these things. There is still hope we can make the world a better place.

Growing up in a small town in Utah, I was sheltered from a lot of things happening in the world. My father went through the Great Depression and World War II when he was a child. His generation was humbled by the events of the world and struggled to bring about peace and prosperity to an uncertain future. There hope brought about our present. It is our hope that will bring about our grandchildren's future.

How do we want to leave the world when we go? What will our generation leave for the next generation? I grew up with people talking about the end of war, the end of poverty, and the end of suffering for the people of the world. We have the ability to do this. We have the ability to health the earth and to bring about peace and prosperity to the world.

We live in a time were technology can take us to Mars and beyond, were no one has to go hungry, were wars can be the thing of the past, were we have unlimited knowledge at our fingertips. It is an amazing time to live, an amazing time to be able to experience life. When I was growing up, I thought it would be neat to be able to go to different parts of the world. Today this is possible. There are only a handful of places where war and violence prohibits people from visiting.

Peace

Peace is obtainable. There are some countries like Syria, Afghanistan, North Korea, and others that are unstable, but with the cooperation and help from the nations of the world peace can be achieved. If countries can meet together with the United Nations and come together to make an agreement for the Earth with the Paris agreement, the world can come together to make a plan for world peace. It is as simple as that.

The superpowers of the world are in a position to resolve differences and force smaller belligerent countries to arrange a peace agreement. The United Nations can take the lead and enforce the peace in many of the countries of the world and do it with the teeth of the superpowers.

The idea of nationalism is good when people take pride in their country and celebrate their cultural identity, but it can be a bad thing when nationalism is about competing with other countries and putting a nation higher than other nations. Many wars were fought over because of nationalism. Germany during both World Wars is an example of this.

We can achieve world peace within a decade, but it does require sacrifice from countries and people to lay aside petty differences. Instead of making disputes over territory and political ideology countries need to look for ways of negotiation and cooperation. Countries can look at win win situations where both countries benefit from agreements and no one has to compromise. Everyone benefits if they work together instead of fighting.

Prosperity

Farmers can grow enough food to feed the world and still have a surplus. If countries cooperated with each other they could produce enough food to be able to have some reserve for times when there is a drought or environmental crisis. There may be a time when this will happen and we would be ready if we worked together. But without cooperation when the crisis hits many people will starve.

In the past it was the distribution of food that was a problem. Today food can be shipped just about anywhere and get to people who need it within 24 hours. There is still problems with the cooperation of governments and the food ends up not getting where it is needed, but this can be easily resolved with the cooperation of governments.

There is a possibility of changing the economy of the world, so that there would be no need for trade disputes or taxes between countries. Free trade can be a global concept one that benefits everyone especially people who need lower prices to obtain things. Countries can still maintain their autonomy and belong to a world wide economic federation. This economic federation can bring about prosperity to the world and end poverty.

Peace

World peace is possible. The majority of the people in the world want peace. It is only those small power hungry groups that create war within countries. There needs to be a drastic reversal in thinking when it comes to peace. The present thought is that countries need to maintain a large military force to deter the threat of war. It is true that power hungry dictators need to be held in check through force, but a military mindset just causes more violence and war. Gandhi's non-violence resistance movement in India brought about India's independence. It also worked with the civil rights movement in the Untied States and the lifting of apartheid in South Africa.

There can be no peace in the war until the tools of war are destroyed and people get ride of pride, hate, and thirst for wealth and power. Children need to be taught peace not war. The people of the world need to stand up to the bullies of the world and say, "No more"!

Happiness

Happiness comes from unselfish service to others. It does not come from getting a nice car, living in a nice home, or making a lot of money. It does not come from fame, power, or popularity. People who are wealthy, famous, and have a lot of power will admit they are often miserable with their life and feel unfulfilled.

It is true people who live in poverty, have no friends, and experience pain, abuse, and neglect are also miserable. Yet even in the lowest of neighborhoods there are very happy people who live in loving families and have a heart of gold as they seek to care for others. There are also people who are wealthy and famous who are happy because they too have a loving family and seek to give to others.

The suffering of the world needs to be taken care of by those who can help. Countries, businesses, organizations, and people from all walks of life need to come together in harmony to help each other. It is only when people are living in harmony with each other and who care for each other that happiness can take place. Happiness is in the smile of a child, the beauty of flowers, the sounds of laughter, and the tend hug of a friend.

Hope

The world has a lot of problems. It has always had problems throughout history. Many of these problems we have worked to solve like many diseases. We can over the problems we face in the world today. It may take baby steps, but it can be done. We need to start moving forward, before the hope fades. Now is the time to do these things. There is no other time in history where we are on the verge of being able to solve most of the world's problems. Diseases like cancer, heart disease, diabetes, can become a thing of the past. Contagious diseases like HIV, cholera, and measles can be eradicated.

Life as we know it can be transformed into something magical. We owe it to our grandchildren and their grandchildren. We need to leave a legacy that saves the planet from human involvement, a legacy of world peace and stopping poverty and hunger. In the spirit of global cooperation and effort there is no problem that cannot be solved.